happiness is ...
快樂就是……

快樂就是……

500種表達我愛你的方式

《快樂就是……》第3集

happiness is ...

500 Ways to Show I Love You

麗莎·史瓦琳 & 拉夫·羅拉薩

Lisa Swerling & Ralph Lazar

著

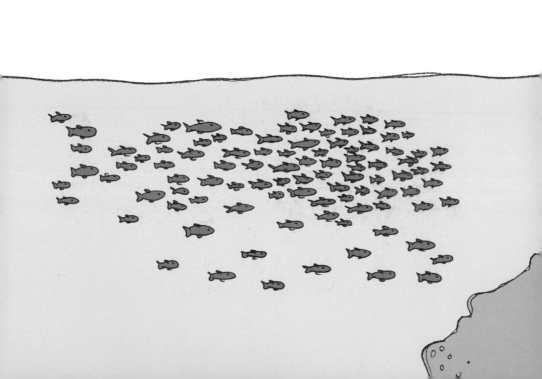

discovering new worlds
一起發現新世界

trusting you
completely
完全信任你

getting ready for the
day together
一起準備新的一天

being the small spoon
依偎在你的懷把裡

being understanding
理解對方感受

celebrating your
success
為你的成就感到高興

getting my hair cut
the way you like it

把頭髮剪成
你喜歡的樣子

being on the same side
我們是一國的

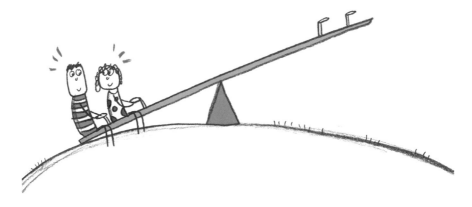

helping each other with work-life balance
互相幫助，平衡彼此的工作與生活

standing up for you
挺身而出為你說話

seeing the world through a similar lens
我們用相似的角度看這個世界

a kiss through the phone
電話裡傳來啵的一聲吻

mapping out our life together
一起規劃我們的人生

looking at each other and cracking up for no reason
我看著你，你看著我，
沒什麼原因，就笑出來了

12

sharing a sunset
一起看夕陽

finding our
dream home
找到我們
夢想的家

拍賣

appreciating your patience
喜歡你這麼有耐心

talking late into the night
晚上聊到很晚

our stupid inside jokes
只有我們倆才懂的蠢笑話

a laughter attack for no reason
不為什麼，兩人就一直笑一直笑

feeling excited when your
name pops up on my phone
你的名字從手機上跳出來，
就覺得好高興

relaxing at the
end of a tiring day
結束了疲憊的一天，
休息一下

stability
穩定交往中

hearing your voice
聽見你的聲音

that electric touch
有種觸電的感覺

rushing out of work to meet you
趕著下班，只為了見到你

Romeo & Juliet
像羅蜜歐與茱麗葉那樣

being more excited about
your birthday than my own
你生日到了，我比自己
過生日還高興

escaping from the
crowd
和你暫時遠離人群

tucking you in
幫你蓋好被子

facing the world together
一起面對這個世界

a sushi date
和你來個壽司約會

sharing the good and the bad
是福是禍，共同度過

telling you you're beautiful
跟你說，你好美

23

taking a risk because I'm with you
有你在身邊，就敢冒險

an unplanned date
臨時約一約，我們就出發了

*getting a letter
from you*
收到你寄來的信

our engagement ring
我們的訂婚戒指

25

pointing out little sweet things to each other
看到可愛的小東西，就指給對方看

making the coffee
just how you like it
知道你喜歡什麼樣的咖啡，
泡給你喝

taking a great selfie
together
拍一張好棒的自拍照

thinking of you all
the time
一直想到你

going au naturel

跟你一起裸體

being cheek to cheek
臉貼臉

never losing our
youthful glow
常保年輕活力

encouraging each other's creativity
彼此鼓勵，發揮創意

being your partner in crime
就算你做壞事，我也跟著

teaching each other new things
彼此教導新鮮事物

showing you that
I'm hilarious
把自己最爆笑的一面
秀給你看

our own secret recipes
專屬我倆的祕密食譜

you looking cute in
my sweater
穿著我的毛衣，你看起來好美

splitting the housework
分工做家事

just being
ourselves
自在做自己

sharing a meal outside
在戶外享用大餐

buying you too many gifts
買了超多的禮物要送你

encouraging
your appetite
鼓勵你多吃一點

packing for a trip together
為了我倆的旅遊一起打包

realizing you're "the one"
猛然發現：你就是我的真命伴侶

feeling like an unbeatable team
覺得我倆是天下無敵的隊友

being married to
your best friend
和最要好的朋友
共結連理

exploring new horizons
探索未知的新疆界

slow dancing
跳一支慢舞

our special spot
只和你共享的角落

40

knowing you're there for me
深知你會接住我

perfecting a super-annoying
wake-up routine
精通了一種超討人厭的起床儀式

realizing how much I love you
瞭解到我愛你有多深

appreciating your thoughtfulness
感受到你的體貼

communication,
without words
無須言語也能溝通

driving for hours to see you
開了大老遠的車，只為見你一面

splurging on a
fancy hotel
花大錢住昂貴旅館

44

sharing hobbies
有相同的嗜好

making you smile
逗你笑

giggling in bed till late
在床上傻笑著直到半夜

getting lost on purpose
故意迷路

finding a book that reminds me of you
無意中看到一本書，讓我想起了你

making a list of the
places we've traveled
列出我們一起去過的地方

being happy for you
為你感到高興

watching the seasons change
季節就在我們眼前變換

when you lift me up
while hugging
抱著我，把我舉高

writing a poem for you
為你寫了首詩

discovering new places together
一起發現從來沒去過的地方

49

solving problems together
一起解決問題

giving you a longer back
rub than you gave me
幫你按按背，比你幫我按摩
的時間還要久

unwavering devotion
從一而終，恆久不改

you and me and the
great outdoors
只有你，我，大自然

being inseparable
如膠似漆

seeing your name in
my email inbox
看見你的名字出現在
信箱的「寄件人」那邊

stopping for junk food on a road trip
開車出去玩的時候，停下來買垃圾食物

falling in love with a new city together
我們同時愛上一個陌生的城市

sleeping in your shirt
睡覺時穿著你的襯衫

watching your
favorite movie for
the tenth time
第十次和你一起重看
你最愛的電影

staying in love
through it all
經歷風雨，
依然相愛

being true to our
childlike hearts
保持童心

never saying "I told
you so" even when I
told you so
雖然我早就告訴過你了，
但我從不對你說
「我早就告訴你了！」

being on the same wavelength
我們倆的波長是相同的

realizing how
lucky we are
我們知道，
我們真的很幸運

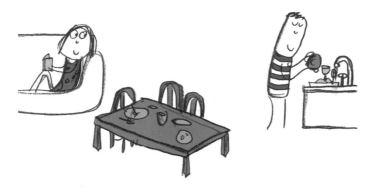

doing little favors for each other
幫對方一個小忙

waking up beside you
在你身旁醒來

57

lying next to you in peaceful silence
躺在你身邊，什麼也不用說

surprising you with
flowers
送你一把花，讓你驚喜一下

giving you a push
when you need it
推你一把，在你需
要的時刻

quiet weekday evenings
平靜的週間晚上

a sweet goodnight text
甜蜜的晚安簡訊

smiling stupidly because a
song reminds me of you
聽到一首歌讓我想起你，
我就傻傻的笑了

doing the dishes, even when it's your turn
我來洗碗，雖然今晚輪到你

watching the big game with you
和你一起收看重要賽事

making a wish about our future
為了我倆的未來許願

treating ourselves
好好款待我們自己

covering you up when
you fall asleep
你睡了，替你蓋好被子

Jack & Rose
來玩《鐵達尼號》！

remembering an
anniversary
記得我們的週年紀念日

finding our way
我們找到了方向

tickling you then running away
搔你癢，然後跑開

romantic gestures
做浪漫的事

hearing your
heartbeat
聽著你心跳的聲音

knowing all of your best stories
你的每一個好友我都認識

scaring the living daylights out of you
把你嚇了超大一跳

humming along to one of our favorite songs
跟著哼我們倆喜愛的歌曲

watching the clouds
看雲

rocking our bed heads
晃著一頭剛起床的亂髮

always making plans for our next vacation
一直在規劃下一次的假期

a random wink
沒事擠眉弄眼一下

getting you the perfect gift
送你一個超棒的禮物

dreaming of you
夢見你

finding our way back to each other
回到彼此的懷抱

having cute nicknames
for each other
互相幫對方取可愛的綽號

always saving
you a spot
一定會替你
留個位子

getting butterflies when I see you
只要看到你，我心裡就小鹿亂撞

when opposites
attract
相互吸引的時刻

watching you realize your dreams
見證你實現夢想的那一刻

spoiling you rotten
寵你溺愛你什麼都給你

when your smile
makes everything ok
你一笑，萬事都ok

73

being ridiculous
在一起胡鬧

listening to our song
聽我們的歌

when you grab my hand
你牽著我

decluttering to make
room for what's important
為了容納更重要的東西，
把家裡清理乾淨

blowing you a kiss
拋個飛吻給你

giving you the heart
of my artichoke
把最好的給你

simple coexistence
在一起就好

watching the moon rise
看著月亮升起

letting you show off
讓你好好大顯身手

sleeping under the stars
在星空下共枕

being joined at the hip
形影不離

having our own
definition of sanity
幹著瘋狂的事

planning for
our future
規劃我們的未來

believing in you,
always
永遠相信你

letting our
hearts lead us
跟著感覺走

making your
favorite snack
做你最喜歡的點心

when you look after me in
awkward social situations

在令人不自在的社交場合，有你照顧我

making memories

創造回憶

turning a house into a home
把住處變成我們的家

being alone together
只有你和我

letting go
放掉一切

acting like an idiot
to cheer you up
要寶逗你開心

*your little
snoring noises*
你發出輕微的
鼾聲

enjoying the simple
moments
共享單純的時刻

getting lost in time with you
與你在一起，忘了時間

an indoor picnic

來場室內野餐

working side by side
一起工作

having a shared mission
共同做一件事

sneaking out of the party
偷偷溜出派對

*waking up in
your arms*
在你的臂彎醒來

finding calm waters with you
和你到風平浪靜之處

*being perfect
travel companions*
最佳的旅伴

sharing an unforgettable view
共享一個難忘的景致

building something amazing together
一起創建一個很棒的事物

appreciating
your cooking
很感激你做菜

exploring
together
一塊兒探險

being your chauffeur
我當你的司機

tolerating your
eccentricities
容忍你的怪

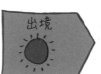

breaking the rules
不守規矩

a romantic candlelit
dinner for two
雙人浪漫燭光晚餐

being in it together
無論什麼事，兩人共度

just us and the open road
兩個人，前途寬廣

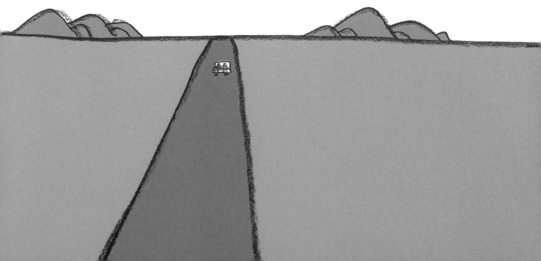

letting the little
things go
不把小事放在心上

catching our dinner
為晚餐出力

one glass, two straws
共喝一杯飲料

knowing I have the best
partner of all
我有最棒的隊友

reading together in
a quiet house
在安靜的房內共讀

getting our first pet
我們的第一隻寵物

you popping onto
my desktop
你出現在筆電螢幕上

learning your recipes
跟你學做菜

trying new things with you
和你一塊嘗試新事物

becoming parents
我們當父母了！

humoring you when you're
lost but won't admit it
你迷路又不願承認的時候，
消遣你一下

carving our first
pumpkin together
一起刻出我們第一個
萬聖節南瓜

a long autumn stroll
秋意正濃，好好散個步

a kiss chase
追著你玩親親

finding shelter
找到一個遮風避雨的地方

disregarding consequences
管他的

getting on a plane to see you
大老遠搭機來看你

sharing a home
共享一個家

helping you chase your dreams
幫你追夢

夢想⋯⋯

an empty beach and us
與你同在無人的海灘

being on the ride of our lives
一起踏上人生的旅程

fantasizing about our
dream home
幻想著我們夢想中的家園

relaxing by the fire
在爐火邊放輕鬆

our family traditions
我們的家庭傳統

*breaking into a
random race*
突然間我們就追逐起來

weathering storms together
風雨共度

you, me, and the cats
有你，有我，有貓

loving our crazy family
愛著我們這瘋狂的
這一家子

making you a cup
of tea just when
you need it
你需要的時候，
為你泡一杯茶

playing around like kids
像孩子般玩耍

watching hours of tv with you
和你一起看好幾小時的電視

introducing you to all my friends
把你介紹給我的朋友

two of us, one piece
of cake
兩個人，一片蛋糕

teasing you
捉弄你

being given space
when you need it
給你一些空間

being impressed by
how cool you are
你的酷，讓我印象好深

a little healthy competition
來點有益健康的比賽吧

a lazy weekend together
慵懶地共度週末

*feeling fearless when
we're together*
有你同在，就覺得
無所懼怕

late-night strolls
在深夜散步

enduring your
latest obsessions
你最近迷上了什麼，
我都能接受

showing you
a book I love
告訴你我喜歡的書

getting cozy in
cold weather
天寒地凍時，
幹點瘋狂的事

大蒜　　愛　　朋友　　陽光　　　笑容
瘋狂　　家　　音樂　　健康　　　乳酪
書　　　自由　高山　　家人　　　寵物
我的床　藝術　電影　　　　　　週末
微笑　夕陽　意識　　烤麵包機

counting our blessings
數算著那些讓我們
感到幸福的事物

finding treasures in our storage unit
在儲藏室挖到寶

knowing just what to say
不要說錯話

a shared life
共享生命

rushing out to the dance floor
when our song comes on
我們的歌一播出，
就衝進舞池

a soft touch
溫柔的碰觸

giving you my undivided attention
把我所有的心力都給你

staring into your eyes
凝視你的雙眸

a fun double date
好玩的兩對情侶約會

always making time to
see each other
為了見到對方，
永遠有時間

falling asleep at the same time
同時睡著

growing your own little garden
栽種屬於你的小花園

imagining spending the
rest of our lives together
想像與你共度此生

discovering your
hidden talents
發現你好有才華

fireside chats
爐邊談天

sharing the same interests
志趣相投

helping you find your
keys ... again
老是在幫你找鑰匙

misbehaving once in a while
偶爾淘氣一下

freedom
自由！

adding special touches
to our house
為家裡妝點增色

knowing you're always
just a phone call away
只要一通電話，就找得到你

a party for two
雙人派對

flashing a grin to
diffuse a situation
要發飆了，趕快陪笑

slowing down to enjoy the view
放慢速度，欣賞風景

not having a care
in the world
管他世間雜事

getting lost in an
activity together
一起專注做著某事

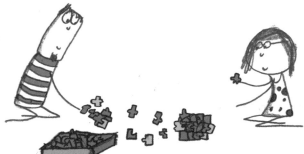

making you something
做一件東西給你

*thanking you for something
I often take for granted*
不再視為理所當然，
而是衷心感謝

coming home to a big smile
after a hard day at work
累了一天，家裡有個燦爛的
微笑等待著我

playing hooky
together
相約蹺課去

putting old photos in an album and
reliving every moment
把老照片放進相簿，一起回味

getting a package
from you
收到你寄來的包裹

135

when I catch you looking at me
瞄到你在偷看我

when plans are
canceled and we get
to stay in
計畫取消，待在家裡

dressing up in a
couple's costume
穿起情侶裝

making up after
a bad fight
大吵一架，重修舊好

出境

taking off on an
adventure
出發去冒險

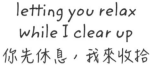

letting you relax
while I clear up
你先休息，我來收拾

reflecting back
沈浸在回憶中

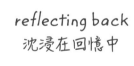

realizing I am completely and
utterly in love
一種「完完全全在戀愛中」
的感覺

giving you the
biggest slice
把最大份的給你

a fondue night
起士鍋之夜

hearing your car pulling
up outside
門外傳來你停車的聲音

bugging you when
you're grumpy
你心情不好的時候，
一直來煩你

late-night snacking
吃宵夜

an impromptu picnic
臨時起意去野餐

taking a rest when you need it
累了，就休息一下

writing our initials in the sand
在沙灘上留名

免稅店

出境

buying a souvenir to remember the trip
買個紀念品，為這次旅遊做個留念

just walking along in silence
只是安靜地散步

loving the sound of your laugh
喜歡你笑的聲音

※火爆浪子

Sandy & Danny
玩角色扮演

143

being in sync
默契十足

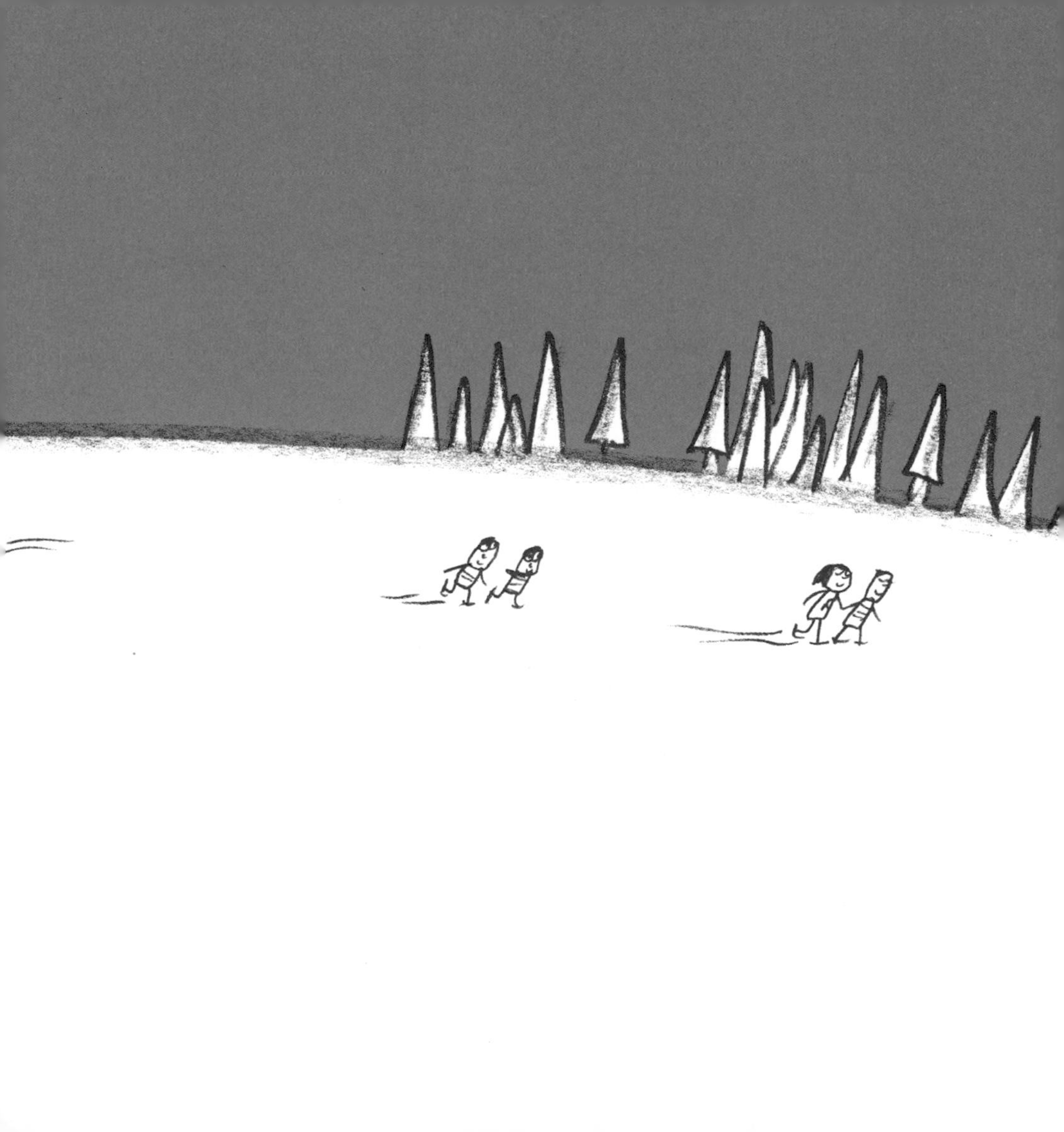

having fun
玩耍

finding the perfect card for you
找到一張卡片，超適合送給你的

spending the whole
day together
一整天都形影不離

being spontaneous
自動自發照顧你

a comfortable silence
among all the chatter
在嘈雜聲當中，享受寧靜

taking wild
rides together
玩到瘋

picking a flower for you
摘一朵花給你

picking you up at the airport
去機場接你

a photo of us on the fridge
冰箱門上貼著我們倆的合照

taking the trip of a lifetime
一生一次的旅遊

a long coastal drive
沿著海岸開呀開

mending a rift
彌平了嫌隙

walking
arm in
arm
手挽著手
走路

sharing a suitcase
把兩人的東西裝進
同一個旅行箱裡

bringing you a box
of chocolates for no
reason in particular
沒特別原因，就送你
一盒巧克力

setting up camp
紮營

concocting
your favorite
beverage
調一杯你最愛
的飲料

going along with your
crazy plans
不管你的計畫多瘋狂，
我一定一起

154

being together in any weather
無論天氣好壞，就是在一起

jumping in
撩落去

working as a team
一起合作

heading out together with no destination
沒目的地，就一起出發了

getting to know you
越來越認識你

loving your weird relatives
你們家人好奇怪喔，但我還是愛他們

a romantic
getaway
浪漫的假期

being first to apologize
先開口道歉

dressing up just for you
為了你裝扮

an emotional reunion
令人情緒激動的團圓

seeing how cute you
are in the morning
瞧你早上剛起床的
可愛模樣

saying yes
說出，我願意

buying our
first car
買下我們的
第一輛車

never letting life get between us
不讓日常瑣事干擾到我們

inviting you into my family
邀你認識我的家人

checking off our bucket list
一塊完成人生的心願

riding a bicycle built for two
兩人騎著腳踏車

162

getting caught in the rain
遇上一陣雨

looking at photos
from when we
first met
看著我們初次相遇
的照片

wishing upon a startogether
一起對星星許願

**ensuring you're nice
and warm**
確認你有沒有穿好穿暖

John & Yoko
我們就像約翰藍儂
和小野洋子

**making you laugh so hard you spit
out your drink**
讓你笑到飲料都噴出來了

*a tight hug after a
heated argument*
我們發狠狂吵，然後
緊緊擁抱

trying new foods together
一起嘗試沒吃過的東西

raising a family
經營一個家庭

knowing each other's
thoughts
連對方心裡在想什麼都知道

telling you that you're
the best thing that ever
happened to me
我跟你說喔，這輩子最棒
的事就是遇見你

the sound of you
breathing
你呼吸的聲音

169

when you insist on walking on the
traffic side of the sidewalk
你堅持走在外側，幫我擋車

saying "I love you" for the first time
第一次說「我愛你」

bragging about your
accomplishments
向友人吹噓你有多厲害

an eskimo kiss
來個愛斯基摩式的
鼻子親親

feeling blessed to have you
有你，真是福氣

escaping for the day
暫離塵囂

feeling comfortable with
you no matter what
無論怎樣，和你在一起
就是自在

the smell of your hair
你的髮香

a toast in a
magical setting
在奇妙的地方，
舉杯互祝

making you a cake
為你做個蛋糕

going over the top
to amuse you
盡我所能讓你快樂

helping each other over obstacles
相互協助，共度難關

making promises
許下承諾

our silly little rituals
我倆專屬的小小儀式，蠻蠢的

178

being celebrated
as a couple
我們的關係受到
大家肯定

having fun just
doing errands
together
只是和你外出辦個
小事，也很開心

getting each other safely to the other side
彼此扶持，直到彼岸

sleeping late
睡到自然醒

going for it
跳吧

rereading your
old messages
重讀你以前
傳來的訊息

seeing you get a tad jealous
發現你有點吃醋

loving the same team
支持同個球隊

feeling protected
被保護的感覺

telling the story of how we met
說著我們認識的經過

heading in the same direction
方向一致

just chillin'
來涼一下

getting that little
something off your
cheek
幫你拂掉臉頰上的
小東西

framing our important pictures
把我倆重要的照片裱框起來

laughing at stupid reality shows
看著愚蠢的實境秀發笑

telling you what I
admire about you
告訴你我崇拜你的地方

five minutes of
extra snuggle time
依偎在你身邊,
再五分鐘就好

being us!
做自己

taking the road less traveled
踏上人跡罕至之路

when you bat your
eyelashes
你眨眼示愛

愛你

saying "I love you" in another language
用外國話告訴你「我愛你」

reconnecting after being apart
分離之後重新聯絡上

starting the day in a positive way
積極正向地展開新的一天

letting you win
故意輸給你

finding a treat
you've left me
找到你留給我的
好東西

a really
good kiss
好好
吻一下

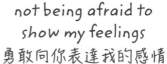

not being afraid to
show my feelings
勇敢向你表達我的感情

a special night out
晚上特別的約會

harvesting what we planted
收成我們栽種的

the snort you do
when laughing
你笑的時候發出的
噴氣聲

knowing that we're
in this together
一起同甘共苦

making you
something by hand
親手製作一個東西
送給你

taking charge
of our lives
我們的人生，
我們作主

watching the world go by,
and thinking of you
看著窗外景象流逝，想著你

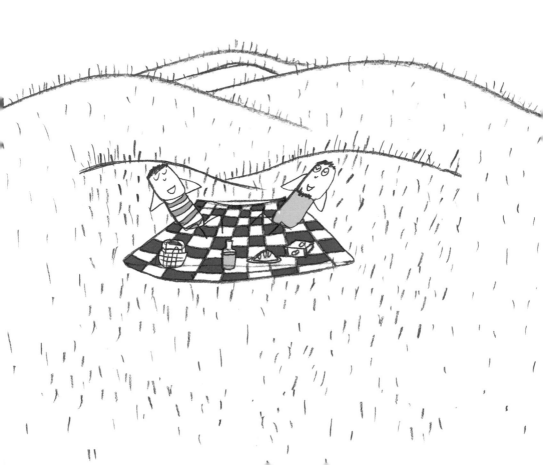
reminiscing
回想

little acts of chivalry
小小的體貼

celebrating in style
很特別的慶祝

knowing I'm going to
see you later
等下就要見面了

Saturday adventures
週六的探險

loving our mutual friends
喜歡我們共同的朋友

reading the paper
together for hours
好幾個小時
一起讀報紙

being on cloud nine
嗨翻天

tolerating your
fashion sense
接受你的時尚感

being inspired by your
example
你做什麼，我跟著做

a lazy Sunday
懶洋洋的禮拜天

the turning point
between a friendship
and a relationship
從單純友誼到確定交往，
那個關鍵轉折點

getting equally enthusiastic
about fancy cheese
我們倆都好喜歡各種各樣
的起司

accepting
imperfections
接受不完美

playing the same tune
琴瑟和鳴

a feeling of awewhen we're together
我們在一起的時候，一股崇敬的感覺油然而生

booking our dream trip
夢想的旅程，下訂了喔

making sure our life's one big adventure
確定我們人生的這場大探險

_tolerating
your musical
aspirations_
你的音樂夢,
我可以忍耐

a great meal with our family
與家人共享一頓美好餐點

leaning on
each other
我們依偎著

helping you have more fun
幫你找到更多樂趣

going the extra mile to
make things special
盡一切努力，讓特別的
事發生

having a bun in the
oven
我們要有小寶寶了！

riding the ups and downs
高山低谷，一路同行

being in our own little world
在我們的小世界裡

sharing nature's wonder
共享自然的奇蹟

admiring your originality
欣賞你的創意

feeling totally content when you're home
你在家我就心滿意足

not minding your little
mood swings
不在意你心裡的
小不爽

tossing away our
worries
拋開煩惱

wearing matching
jammies
我們的睡衣好搭喔

215

just running free
自由自在地奔跑

a long beach walk
漫步在海灘

distracting you
故意搗蛋

loving the way you
describe things
喜歡你描述事情的樣子

staying forever young
永保年輕

knowing we have it really good
我們一切都非常好

acting like total
nutcases for no
reason in particular
無緣無故我們就起肖

getting books for you
from the library
替你去圖書館借書

watching the rain with
you at my side
你在我身旁，我們在看雨

making your happiness
my priority
我最重要的事，就是
讓你快樂

a wish that comes true
願望成真

having fun in the dark
在黑暗中玩遊戲

being regulars
at the local
pub
我們常去住家
附近的酒吧，
都變成熟客了

never running out of things to
talk about
有說不完的話題

jumping as high as we can
盡量跳高

hanging out
in our pj's
穿著睡衣
在一起

giving you gentle guidance
溫柔地指引你

a promise for
forever
永恆的承諾

warming each
other's feet with
our own
彼此用腳，讓對方
的腳暖活起來

being able to let it all hang out
表露本性

being impressed
by your genius
欣賞你的天分

taking care of you when you're sick
你生病我照顧你

a movie date
相約看電影

Tarzan & Jane
像泰山與珍

feeling like anything
is possible
覺得一切都有可能

sneaking up on you
從背後偷襲你

your wonderful silliness
你那股傻勁好好玩

making the house nice just for you
為了你，把屋子打理得很舒適

still dating even when we're
married
雖然結婚了，還是常約會

being
unconventional
來點另類的

Antony &
Cleopatra
安東尼與埃及豔后

233

happy domesticity
居家生活好快樂

噗！

sharing holidays with you
和你共度假日

keeping you entertained
讓你快活

tolerating each other's midlife crises
忍受彼此的中年危機

waiting for you to get home
等你回家

having the same
obsessions
我們連執念都一樣呢

making a life-changing
decision together
共同做出改變人生的決定

knowing I can tell you anything
我能把所有的事都告訴你

having special secrets
共享特殊的小祕密

seeing you in our kids
從孩子身上，看見你的影子

having a soak
together
一起泡個澡

mastering the
balancing act
我們很會平衡生活

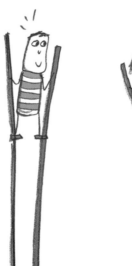

when what we think, what we say, and what we do are in harmony

我們的想法、言語、行動都很配合得剛剛好

finishing
each other's
sentences
我話還沒說完，
你就接上了

A, B, C, D...

E, F, G!

sharing headphones
戴著同一個耳機

feeling the
warmth of
your hand
感覺到你溫暖的手

a stolen kiss
偷偷一吻

breakfast in bed
床上共進早餐

242

experimenting
in the kitchen
together
在廚房做實驗

laughing at your
dumb jokes
被你的蠢笑話逗樂了

dreaming about you,
then waking up smiling
夢中見到你，微笑著醒來

sharing a milestone anniversary
共度一個重要的週年紀念日

sticking together against the odds
逆境中仍然緊緊在一起

a goodnight kiss
晚安之吻

when you're helpful
without being asked
不用我說，你就主動來幫忙

a madcap adventure
傻傻地一起冒險

having the same priorities

想先做的事情都一樣

feeling valued
感覺到自己是被珍惜的

fitting togetherlike
puzzle pieces
緊密契合有如拼圖

Rachel & Ross
有如《六人行》裡
的羅斯與瑞秋圓滿
大結局

夜店

going out late, just
the two of us
很晚了，只有
我們一起出去

saving the last piece
of chocolate for you
把最好的一塊巧克力
留給你

watching our
wedding video
一起看著我們的
婚禮影片

talking for hours even
though we've spent all
day together
一整天都在一起，之後
還能再講好幾個小時

when you don't want to let go
你不願放開我的手

slowing down to smell the roses
放慢腳步，聞著玫瑰芳香

taking much-needed time off
共度一個渴想已久的假期

前往
渡假小島
班機

Elizabeth Bennet &
Mr. Darcy
有情人終成眷屬，有如
《傲慢與偏見》的依莉
莎白與達西先生

being proud
of your
achievements
因你的成就而驕傲

recharging our
batteries together
一起充個電

knowing your taste
曉得你喜歡什麼

being partners
for life
一生相伴

dancing around
the house
在屋裡跳舞

surprising you with your
favorite meal
給你個驚喜，煮一頓
你最愛吃的菜

falling in love
墜入愛河

256

seizing the moment
良辰吉時一定要把握

sharing a meal with a view

美食美景，與你共享

loving the song you
recommended
喜歡你推薦的歌

when you look into my
eyes that way
你用那種特別的方式
深深注視著我

accepting your apology
接受你的道歉

the way you hug
你擁抱的方式

having compassion
你知道我難過

being with you in the kitchen
和你一起在廚房裡

watching you dance
看你跳舞

a spa day for two
兩人一起做spa

feeling cool when we're together
與你在一起，真酷！

knowing we are together in this big, vast world
世界雖大，但我知你與我同行

pulling each other out of the hole,
no matter how deep it gets
無論麻煩多大，彼此協助一起脫困

being swept away
一起飛走

a spontaneous
head scratch
自動幫你抓抓頭

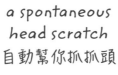

shared indulgences
放縱一下

cheering you up
when you're just at
the end of a sulk
你的氣快消了，
我趕快來逗你開心

making plans for just us!
一起做計畫

goofing around
鬼混一陣子

exploring the world
探索新天地

exchanging little gifts
互贈小禮

sharing a pot of tea
共享一壺茶

admitting you were right all along
承認其實你是對的

remembering when
we were younger
回想以前年輕的日子

understanding that love
is all we need
我們一無所求，
只需要彼此的愛

快樂就是……
500種表達我愛你的方式
《快樂就是……》第3集
happiness is ...
500 ways to Show I Love You

作　者　麗莎史‧瓦琳 (Lisa Swerling) & 拉夫‧羅拉薩 (Ralph Lazar)
行銷企畫　高芸珮
責任編輯　陳希林
封面設計　賴姵伶
內文構成　賴姵伶

發 行 人　王榮文
出版發行　遠流出版事業股份有限公司
地　　址　臺北市南昌路2段81號6樓
客服電話　02-2392-6899
傳　　真　02-2392-6658
郵　　撥　0189456-1
著作權顧問　蕭雄淋律師

2019年07月01日　初版一刷
定　　價　平裝新台幣280元 (如有缺頁或破損，請寄回更換)
有著作權‧侵害必究　Printed in Taiwan
ISBN　978-957-32-8541-0
遠流博識網　http://www.ylib.com
E-mail：ylib@ylib.com

國家圖書館出版品預行編目(CIP)資料

快樂就是......500種表達我愛你的方式 / 麗莎.史瓦琳(Lisa
Swerling), 拉夫.羅拉薩(Ralph Lazar)著 -- 初版. -- 臺北市
: 遠流, 2019.07
面；　公分. -- (快樂就是系列；3)
譯自：Happiness is... : : 500 ways to show i love you
ISBN 978-957-32-8541-0(平裝)

1.愛 2.通俗作品

199.8　　　　　　　108005005